Every Substance Clothed

Every Substance Clothed

POEMS BY

Kathleen Halme

❧

For Carolyn,
Who knows the
iamb's deepest beating
pulse. Fondly,
Kathleen

Feb. 26, 2009
Palio in sunshine

The University of Georgia Press

Athens and London

Published by the University of Georgia Press
Athens, Georgia 30602
© 1995 by Kathleen Halme
All rights reserved

Designed by Betty Palmer McDaniel
Set in 10.5 on 13 Berkeley Oldstyle Medium
The paper in this book meets the guidelines for
permanence and durability of the Committee on
Production Guidelines for Book Longevity of the
Council on Library Resources.

Printed in the United States of America

95 96 97 98 99   P   5 4 3 2 1

Library of Congress Cataloging in Publication Data
Halme, Kathleen.
Every substance clothed : poems / by Kathleen Halme.
p. cm.
ISBN 0–8203–1762–4 (pbk.: alk. paper)
I. Title.
PS3558.A3955E94   1995
811´.54—dc20   95–13566

British Library Cataloging in Publication Data available

For Alan

That is lofty, steep, uneven, and arduous:
This is sloping, gentle, soft, and pleasing.

ANDREW MARVELL,
"Epigram on Two Mountains, Almscliff
and Bilbrough: To Fairfax"

Acknowledgments

Grateful acknowledgment is made to the editors of the publications in which the following poems, several in different versions, first appeared:

American Voice: "Carnivores," "A Celibate Imagination," Delilah in Dixie," "Desire Lines," and "The Everlasting Universe of Things"
Blue Ox Review: "You Are Given an Amulet"
Boston Review: "A Small Red Parcel" and "Something New"
Boulevard: "In Silence Visible and Perpetual Calm"
Chaminade Literary Review: "In Situ"
Denver Quarterly: "Diorama Notebook," "The Speaking Face of Earth," and "Incidents and Accidents"
Laurel Review: "The Second Sunday of Easter" and "A World without Words"
Michigan Quarterly Review: "Aspirants and Postulants"
North American Review: "English to English"
Pembroke Magazine: "Nuptial Suite for Signe Saari"
Rackham Journal of the Arts and Humanities: "In a Rooming House for Women Only"
River Styx: "An Appalachian Town: Points of Definition"
So to Speak: "Seul à Seul"
South Carolina Review: "Mary Magdalene's Ideal Christmas"
Southern Poetry Review: "Working Out in the New South"
Virginia Quarterly Review: "The Eloquence of Objects, the Demise of Material Culture" and "Poem with Ethnic Overtones"

New Rivers Press published "Sauna" in *Sampo: The Magic Mill—A Collection of Finnish-American Writing*.

Contents

One

Two

Three

One

Diorama Notebook

1

The very I ants into the museum case of history—diorama, *tableau
    vivant*—
climbs the peasant girl's triple skirts and rests on the pale skin line
of her braided wedding crown, the white road of her head.
The stasis of faked history splayed in smudgeable terms.

2

North is pure delusion, snowblind and rapturous.
Peasant saints abuzz in the miasma,
the presences and outcomes of lexicons,
know how long a dog can bark.

3

Slashers and burners, escape artists, a family sick of the past,
with a name that translates: "burnt-over field sown with grain,"
"he hasn't been seen in these parts for some time."

I want to live in a commonwealth of heroes
where history hasn't lost its nerve.

4

Our matriarch never owned a pair of pants.
She won't speak English or use spoon sugar. She won't turn lights on
when the woods around her stitch up at night,
and now, she must finally leave the farm.

3

Whoever you are, you could buy this life-size diorama
of immigrant life for less than the price of a nice foreign car.

5

My father kept a clean-shaved face.
The week before he was to sail back home to find a wife,
he found my mother at a dance.

The accordion pleats a schodish. Lenin's portrait beams
—a new world saint behind the stage.
My father smiles as though taken by a universal spell.
My mother has saved herself for the wholly invisible.

I see them as a couple on a cake,
moving without moving
for their own sake.

6

Lard in two-pound coffee cans makes a sauna stove burn hard.
When the wooden door slams shut, blood boils in the thick of skin.
Corpuscles scream in heat that might make you think
of old-time words like god and sin.

7

I have been a bride, a wave motion of crinoline,
have seen the broken strand of pearls wash away in waves.
What does the partner want—to make a new wife out of gold?

I have watched men shave and taken them to bed.
Lovers with seams, have you stayed stitched? night
Oh, the wholly naked sex. We lather in the new world mess.

4

Leave the homestead unlocked, unboarded,
and tell the flannel town the credenza's full of bric-a-brac.
Let them wake up spoons and pull the needle
through the lace. Let them strop the double blade
and shave the window frame. Let the townkids liquor up
and hump the metal beds. Let hunters fire through the floor.
When the table burns, let them burn the door.
Douse the husk with gas and let it finger flames.
Let the dead line up and laugh, still awkward in America.

The Speaking Face of Earth

Snow was my cartouche, illiterate's paper.
I shaped breasts on angels and devil horns.

I sucked on snow and drank its metal down.
Inside summer's freezer, by frozen deer meat bundles,

hard-packed snowballs shrunk to hosts.
I bit down hard like a mammal with a god.

Sweet Things

No girl went to Joe Karni's store alone.
Stuck under bunches of bad bananas
and bruised peaches, pointy bras in boxes,
dusty kites bound tight to pine sticks, hid
secrets big enough to feel.

One day in an old summer, my sister and I
rode our Schwinns to Joe's. "Pick 'em out!"
he yelled as we raked through
sticky Mary Janes and Nickel Sips.
He watched us through the candy case.

"Let's go," I whispered to my sister.
She combed a box of hard candy—
ribbons, raspberries, peanuts—leftovers
from Christmas. As she followed me up front to pay,
I saw Joe's room behind the butcher case.

His t.v. was turned on without sound.
I saw a baby doll standing by itself.
Still, we dumped our bags in front of him.
He flicked the candies as he counted them,
he made us take the pennies from his palm.

Like coming out of a double matinee,
we blinked, rubbery and blind. We kicked up
our stands, pedaling fast, snapping
the air with licorice whips, kissing
the air with red wax lips.

Salinity

I grew up on an inland ocean
and licked unsalted stones,
then skipped them over Superior,
the only Great Lake I'd known.

Deer came to lick the salt block in our field.
Slender, intent, they made the pillar disappear.
In secret, I licked the new block in our barn;
the burn was formal, illustrative.

I went swimming with a boy to touch him underwater.
In the reeds I licked the salt flame off his chest.
Through no fault of our own, we are called
to ocean, called to salt and called alone.

Incidents and Accidents

Grave materialist, she dives into the women's pool.
The water laps her recent breasts. Last night
she was his hand of water turning warm to touch.

"Mammal," she thinks, volting past the standing mother
in the swimming lane, swears *she* won't get mummered
like those others. The woman, runneled floral, doesn't budge.

A clot of black cloud rumbles to the west.
Seeded and resplendent, water breaks
on water, over one, over everyone.

The Eloquence of Objects,
the Demise of Material Culture

Upper Peninsula Michigan Household, Circa 1963:
Winter dresses up early for Halloween.
I have to wear a snow suit under my devil costume—
I almost stay at home and read. I read the real
estate page. Where are these estates
in our tar-paper county—why do the ads try
to convince us every day that these are <u>real</u> estates?
I hide words in pockets of my first blue jeans—
red flannel lined, sent from Sears.

At home we have a Bible with pictures of sad people
in robes and wild hair. Only Samson and Delilah interest me.
I'm up to C's in *World Book*, generally a disappointing set.
The librarian downtown lets me bring in penny candy.
My mother never says a word about the romance
novels I read until I'm pale. These books make me think
I'm going to live a lot of love. Sometimes I join my family
in black and white at our console t.v. sent from Sears.

I never see my father read a book. He makes up
stories to tell us about the whales he saw
when he was crossing over from Finland, about the black bear
chasing him home from school—nature stuff like that.
He reads *Outdoor Life* out loud.
"This Happened to Me" is my favorite part.
Some guy almost drowns in a fast river when his hip boots fill up—
then he lives to write about it.

One afternoon I notice a page turned over in the catalog.
A package arrives: frog-green hip boots sent from Sears.

He tells my mother he'll only wear them in
knee-deep water out at Cheney Lake.

November: my father reads in the *Ironwood Daily Globe*
that JFK is coming—one hundred miles away to Ashland.
He takes *us*.
The helicopters chop the air so hard my braids lift off my chest.
We hold salted nut rolls as the president talks.
My father, a shy, generous man
who cuts meat for a living, gets to shake JFK's hand.

"They saw my Bell and Howell and must have thought
I was a reporter," he says, afterward, flushed. My dad,
who quit school at twelve to run
the family farm, gathers himself up, suddenly
American, on the way home from history.

Our neighbors come over on Saturday night to watch
the home movie my father took with his camera
sent from Sears. Evelyn Lahti says, giggling, "Jack Kennedy
is too handsome to be president!" and Toivu Lahti wants
to shake my father's hand. The camera eye flutters
through the bundled crowd and leaves out every word.

The next week at Central School Miss Anderson sobs
in front of our class and tells us the news. "Pray,"
she whispers and lets us go. Walking home I say the word—
assassination, assassination—it whips and hisses
over cracks. At home my mom is actually home—that means
she's working nights again and will smell like ether
in the mornings—she pushes an iron slowly
like a brick, but there's nothing on the board. She doesn't want
to talk; she gives me a sad look, whispers "pray."

I leave her alone to find something to hold.
I get out the Sears catalog and look
at shapes and words: Seeded Voile, Armoire, Chifforobe,
Half Slip, 36 Inch Vanity, two pages of men looking dumb
in lumpy briefs and saggy boxers, twelve pages
of "Foundations"—women trussed up in nylon, spandex, powernet.
Low Voltage Transformer. Plumb Bob of Solid Brass
in Leather Sheath, Big Top Priscillas with Rod Pockets—things
a girl could use. I love the sound
of Pintle Hooks, Lunette Eyes and Couplers;
whatever they might be or do, I want them.
The book weighs heavy on my lap. I'm suddenly exhausted:
it will take me years to order fact and artifact.

Polyptych: Couches of the Dead

History Has Lost Its Nerve
Wooden girl swing down, swing
up in the hollow of the parlor clock
for the first ones swinging legs
over divan and plush. Our actual girl pets
and twists the satin fringe of "Florida—
the Sunshine State," then picks up "M-O-T-H-E-R,"
an old gift in English from her father to his mother.

Culture Is a Prophylactic
The clock isn't telling time tonight. Time will
come back when her *I am not ethnic* aunt
and her aunt's new husband—
this one drives a Chevrolet—
finish in the sauna house and join them in the living
room, panting, red, and hot. Then, as the ritual of cleansing
directs, it's time for the girl and grandmother
to take their turn.

There Are Dark Causes
She begs her aunt in English: "I won't burn myself.
Please make her let me go alone."
The aunt laughs, cuddles her new man,
and says, "she's got nothing to hide!"
He plays with the ties
on her pink chenille until her nipples show.

For the Primitive, Art Is a Means
But it's not time. The clock sanctions *nature morte*,
grips its sharp doily high on the mahogany radio.
She wants to push the nonrepresentational

buttons she was told *don't touch*: Cairo,
Rome, and Tokyo—places a girl could go.

No one plays the radio,
not even for the polka station out of Ishpeming.

She Wishes To Be Her Own Daughter
It's still not time. The peasant girl in a maroon
scarf kneels to feed her pigeons one by one. She is alone
with them at the pump and looks content. She is made from wool.
Our girl wonders why this picture is called "rug"
when it's hung on a wall. Now, the miniature wooden
sauna takes her in its frame. Her eyes carve the backs of women
beating each other with birch switches. They are big women
with breasts like bananas. They ignore their babies.
They are big women who switch each other's backs.

There Was No Problem of Personal Style
"Bad, bad girl," the voice from the ottoman clucks
in the one English it knows. A doily halo keeps
her perm and doilies guard the armrests. She folds her
hands atop a white, clean cake of soap then reconsiders
and pulls a two-pronged pin, U-shaped and long,
from the tatted snow and shoves it in the chair's soft arm.

In Silence Visible and Perpetual Calm

Tonight, you wash your godless plate and cup
and dry them with a linen cloth,
pick a white mint stamped with X's,
then walk to the sauna house heated
with the best logs in the pile,
sit on the highest bench
where you gave birth, and steam.

You walk back—this time, not locking the house.
You dust the hand mirror on your vanity,
pin curl your hair in crosses
and clip both sets of nails,
stop the cuckoo clock,
and slip in the envelope of bed.
You let night fall down around you,
alone now at your calling into white.

Every Substance Is Clothed

> Their only hope is in arrows, which,
> lacking iron, they sharpen with bone.
>
> TACITUS, *Germania*

History is a clumsy cape:
am I qualified to write this poem?
Signe Saari had grown crooked
teeth like corn disordered on a cob.
That kept her shy and busy all summer.
Must I keep allegiance to the reality stone?
Nothing could be done
to straighten out the natural mess, so she made order
elsewhere. A bar of brown scrubbing soap
fit her hands better than the bleached gloves
she wore under her steel graduation watch
on Sundays. *Is there history in this poem?*
She was Baptist, clean, and straight.
She stitched parachute silk into Sunday dresses
and had been kissed once, in the church kitchen,
pushed up against a cast-iron stove,
by a boy who knew how to move people.
Can the writing hand decipher the unknown?

All summer Signe's knees were red from kneeling
on pineboard, scrubbing bare wood
as though she could scrape knots away.
Have I turned her into an Other, exotic and alone?
Oh, the force of smells
she made disappear: her father's snuff and
musk, the liquor that killed her best brother
at Christmas. *Is this ethnographic*
knowledge known? They said it was

16

an accident. In winter
fear can leap like deer in woods.
Am I qualified to write this poem?

Friday nights, all summer, the other maids gone
to Kresge's and the show—*is this memory, rumor,*   *what's*
or imagination alone?—she'd scrub herself down   *real*
with a sauna brush, and pause before slipping
into white cotton—hold her breasts
as though they were something   *her reality —*
she could call her own.   *her substance*
Is there history in this poem?   *clutched*

17

Nuptial Suite for Signe Saari

Morning
How dumb someone looks pinned with a rose corsage lying
in their coffin. A pragmatic Finnish family, they
decided it was best to bury her before the wedding, save
the relatives two trips. After they had put her down,
we unsheathed single blades of grass; they disinterred her
house. My uncle yelled, "Siggy, come get something," and filled
  the flatbed
of his Ford, took the spinning wheel
they had used to make dog hair yarn during a war, a box
of pointy shoes; he even took her bear live trap. Then he spun
away. I didn't want anything except maybe to go
back to bed, her bed, where we had spent our night
before. In the picture I wanted, she'd lean over us,
smelling like frosting flowers and kiss
us, a couple, good night. They insisted we take
something and plunked a paper suitcase full of spices in our trunk.
I still expect strange trunks to open up
a wave of clove and cardamom.

Afternoon
I tried to iron the wedding veil that wound
around the board like a mammal left tied to a pole.
When I thought the last cousin had swished off
to church, I left myself and cried, but
I had company: Poodle Maki, the dried-out
town drunk, stood in the living room asking if he could
help, meaning it. I loved him fiercely
for that consideration. Down Miles Avenue
to First Lutheran I walked alone, letting that tulle whip

behind as though I were heading out to the Great Lakes.
The wind caved in the hollow bodice of my gown. I didn't
care—I'd bought it for myself on sale at Always and Forever.

Wedding Eve and After
We had found her. Fallen and breathing. Beans burning
in a cheap pot. *Jeopardy* asking loud answers we had
no questions to. She always was the smart one, had a year
at Northern before her dad died and they fished her out
to be a bride. Twenty, like me. I lost her only piece
of jewelry, besides the ring they didn't take: a gold cuff
bracelet her man slipped on when she quit
college. A few years ago I lost it
dancing hard in another pack of strangers.

Poem with Ethnic Overtones

The black boat ride to somebody who looks like me is not big
history. Why we find familiars is not the high felt cap, rose and
black, I soon wished you'd bring for me. Is not the hundred
wheels of rye bread thread on ceiling poles for our first year. Is
not the smoke sauna where you soon said you would like to
scrub my back. Is not the unearthed food: turnips, beets, and
tubers. Dark meat for a nine-month winter. Is not the loom
and rugs, a cow and flax linen—the dark dowry I would have
had to bring. Is not the black pots, heavy as the iron age,
vowels simmering in porridge, our icons wincing in the corner
when their twenty-minute flamesticks died: a pole of skeletal
light yours and mine really lived. Is not my name, which
means *burnt-over field sown with grain*, and yours, which means
nothing but water. Is not my lifelong love of licorice in all its
shapes, and the pocket of your friendly coat filled with the nibs
you offered as a way to talk to me, a stranger, on the open-air
ferry. Is not more than you soon lifting my sticky hand, a leaf
still on the tree, lifting my familiar hand, chanting *Dear, Dear.*

Sauna

When people, cars, and Kelvinators
still had rounded sides,
first married couples,
then anyone, uncoupled,
of one sex,
steamed and beat themselves
with spicy birch—
brusque crustaceans who lived
to dance out of the pot alive.

They met the others in a house
to drown in vowels
I didn't know,
to sit around a table
set with Lutheran coffee
and seven kinds of sweets—
the only excess they allowed
that didn't suffocate or sting.

Glad to be mute,
I vowed to marry soon.
I'd be done with the melting widow women
who weren't embarrassed anymore,
who would search my skinny body
for signs of spring as I popped
bubbles in the metallic paint
on the dripping sauna door.

I loved the place;
I didn't have to talk,
still, the woods around

the sauna and the house
urged dark and foreign words,
an angry sounding tongue.

In bed, at night,
I made up words to use some day.
This is no plan for nostalgia.
My grandfather's gradually
losing his mind.
Is it because of a payday gal
he met in the twenties
in an Alaskan sawmill town?
He never learned English;
he keeps his stories home.
His wife married him because he asked.
She left her house in the woods—
the table set, the closets full.
I go sometimes to see
what else has fallen apart.
The measure of memory is her first
husband's coat still hanging stiff
in the tilting porch.

They have stopped asking,
"Marry?"
And poetry, to them, is no husband,
but they let me sauna alone.

Their past is all necessity and work.
Kalle will slip on the sauna floor and die.
Esteri will mumble in a nursing home
where no one will speak Finnish.
Love and luxury have no claim here.
Only words that work.

Two

English to English

1. Dictation
A perfect word exists. It chooses its object.
When you walk across the winter lake,
the land moves back and back.
Once again you don't know anything.
Here is what there is:
a dog sniffing a fish flipping on the ice;
ice-fishing tip-ups set and no fishermen;
when you reach the promontory—
a spilled bucket of mealy worms
(their maggoty color doesn't make you think of anything);
then the tick of leaves left on trees.
Susurrus is a word.

2. Explication
Man A:
You go to the gallery opening
to watch him watch the people
look at the art about art;
to delight in his delight of women:
the curly-top with a white ribbon
bowed on the side of her head.
At a distance, you too love her in an instant.
And still the image,
the perversity of moment looking for symbol,
still the afterimage attracts you,
and he becomes real only when he's gone.

Man B:
One time you missed his presence so much

you rode to his house, climbed on the window ledge,
looked in.
The obscenity of his objects made you leave.
All the way home you hoped you hadn't left footprints
on the ledge.
He becomes real, all-at-once,
by a texture:
the roughness of his wool coat against your cheek;
by a color:
the stain on his palm after you have eaten
a few berries from his hand.
What is the word for the back of the hand?
We want what we can't understand with our minds.

3. Translation
Remember that time the shadow of light settled around you,
filled your room, you tiny creature,
held you flat against the floor,
as if a huge hand were pressing you down behind the neck,
until you gave in to what was true without you
and to every word that ever failed you.

In Situ

1.

Two shovelbums who love each other unaware
toss up a willowware potsherd—
painted with three birds dancing on a blue bridge—
at a dig on the bank of the Yahara.

Neither claims "historic" as opposed to "prehistoric."
Already the screen has chosen many
scraps of the palimpsest
land to place in
the tired hands
of the couple who stands beyond
the ruling of maps.

Love over love over
love like the cave drawings at Lascaux,
she thinks, and still the same tremor
over hands like his.
Back and forth, back
and forth, coaxing the sifting screen.

2.

Under the pop tops, rusty fishing lures,
and Cracker Jack prizes, time before
our time begins, he thinks.
An artifact is anything
which shows human modification.
He reasons: they should put me on the sifting screen.

3.

Will you come over the curled and wavy hills?
I have a gift for you. I have opened the window
of my cottage to better hear the singing
of bluebirds painted on your present
I now hold as I held your head
the evening before last.

4.

The woman scrubs the potsherd:
The new, the new, the burden of the new that's not new.
"Number 786—blue/white historic ceramic piece
found at seventeen centimeters," she writes.
She sees an empty room filled
by the piece, now part of a whole
pitcher painted with the blue
pointed hats and shoes with curled-up toes with bells,
blue piglets and blue figs.
Wavy rooftops and blue pagodas in bloom.
A blue lace village.
She sees it was a pitcher
acquired entirely for pleasure.

The Vulgar Forms of Present Things

What led you to death?
I am curious about you, homunculus
of a god I haven't met.

You look as though you've been
sleeping in that altar case three hundred years.
Humans sure were smaller then.

Are you embalmed, your corpuscles shrunk
to a nut in vestments, or are you a copy like wax fruit?
Do you get up at night and sip from the aspersorium?

Is your litany voluptuous? In the eyeball
of the world, are we the iris?
You make me ask old questions.

I am curious about you, small saint,
you are so lifelike and moment-stopping.
Tell us, please, how to be, which way to live.

Mary Magdalene's Ideal Christmas

1. Shut-In

While the bats act up in the walls
and the radiator chirps
like a cicada
in the first thrash of winter
you will stay in this house as if forever.
Frosted-in and haunted by the soon-to-visit
ghost of poverty,
you have surrendered to small sickness
because it is something bigger than yourself.
You watch people below on the street
to see if they react to your staring.
Do they?
No, they are busy with the cold.
You don't wonder what he's been doing.
It's enough that the dull wonder of his face
still flickers for you.

2. The Girl Downstairs

You picture last night when the sparkly thing
in number twenty-three
came upstairs in only a man's shirt,
draped herself across the armchair as if
it were the lap of a lover,
pulled the shirt down on one shoulder:
"I love my skin—I've always loved it.
I used to suck on it like this," she said,
sucking on the back of her arm,
"because it tastes like graham crackers."

She wants to give you what you want.
You know what to want.
The clove cigarettes she smokes are dipped in honey.

3. *Do Something Useful in Your Seclusion*

Name the ten plagues after Aaron's rod turned
into a serpent:
Water made blood
Frogs
Gnats
Flies
Death to herds and flocks
Boils and sores
Thunder and hail
Locusts
Darkness
The firstborn slain
Then, the parting of the Red Sea.
In those days everyone saw the hand of god.
But tell yourself that love is no more than the color
for a longing bigger than longing.

4. *Winter*

Below, people are shoveling,
smug because they know what to do.
A woman passes in a molting fur coat.
She looks up and waves to tell you
that love, like old religion, is not an artifact.
All these things you will accept and more:
a bar of olive soap bigger than your grasp
left at your door, six birds sitting in the smoke
of the chimney across the street,
and the limitless waiting that is more than faith,
and winter.

5. Mary Magdalene's Ideal Christmas

I want to have a Christmas with him.
At a roadside motel in DeSoto or Boscobel.
We would read from the Gideon's Bible;
he'd smoke lots of Drum tobacco.
We'd eat sandwiches wrapped in tinfoil,
then walk to town to church
to be surrounded by small-town strangers.
We'd walk back looking for some star;
then each alone at separate beds,
the room filled with the fragrance
of mink oil from our boots,
he'd lie down and slowly turn the thoughts over
as if they were flat stones in his palm,
then turn to me,
and maybe I wouldn't be praying to him.
Let's be near each other
like two people walking down the street.

6. That Night He Interpreted
a Scene from the New Testament

He thinks the scene where Jesus
writes with a stick in the dust—
the only mention of Jesus writing—
is about Jesus having just lost his virginity.
That's why Jesus goes on with the business
about casting the first stone.
You think how it would be to have a pound of nard—
that's oil—poured over your head.
And she wiped his feet with her hair.
Maybe love is the possibility of joyfully
understanding
nothing.

In a Rooming House for Women Only

"I go by moonlight," says a man's voice
below on the bartime street.
Six hours until light brings day.
Again I wonder if the spot on the wall
is the breathstain from years of sleep in this bed.
Perhaps she slept on the right side of her body.

"I am a body or I have a body?"
asks the old, old voice
from the house that's still as a bed.
Two and three floors above the street
ten women sleep facing the wall,
and maybe only I am waiting for day.

Early that day or some day,
tired of the smells and sounds of her body,
she turned away from the wall.
I have been listening for the creature's voice
that loses itself in the street
and doesn't linger in the flower bed.

Mrs. D. says this is a different bed—
a new one she bought since that day
when a crowd gathered on the street
hoping to see an unurgent body.
In the Keenan House there is no voice
that can go through a yard-thick wall.

I am too close to the wall
in this small bed—a twin bed—
until my breathing is broken by his voice

asking as a child asks: "Is it day?"
Close, we are glad to be in a body.
Sometimes we are warm even on the street.

Now a ball is bounced down the street.
I move away from the wall
to be nearer to his body
and know we will be like this in bed
for more than this first day
when we didn't muffle the animal voice.

Mixed breath on the wall over the bed.
Far from the street and far from the day,
we can let the body embrace the voice.

A World without Words

A set of fresh lovers meets for the first
time out of bed at a café. They made some
love without words or used a few
words that took shape from their coupling.
Hear them turn their love, a piece
of cake on a plate, placed here between them. They devour
the whorls they put out the night before. Now
in fear of words they have to lean back
and find fast names for the whole dark ordeal.

The first snow is always the one we go out
just to be in, to have snow surround us
on its way down, and on the ground
we move as slowly as the word *elephant*—obsessed
and wanting for once to have snow
tell us without words about snow. As if
what we said meant anything at all. A thick trunk
pointing to an approximation of what we hope
we mean by tromping through unsigned snow.

Maybe this is why we can become so fond
of the afterevent—the grounds after
the circus has pulled up, the rock
overturned, the morning past a private event
taking shape beneath our bungalow. When everything is
final, vulnerable, then we can call it names.

Seul à Seul

for Julia Kristeva

Despite ourselves, a walk is a naming of sight
invisible sparking around us, a smooth sheath we

can slip right through to the beginning of beauty.
What would you call this color? Mouse gray. This

miniature flower? Bluet. What colors are named
after fruits or maybe before? What's a cowpoke,

a piano window? Then the electric fence, questionable
current in bad weather, numinous in our naming. Are

we claiming the world we're making? Give us
a pond so tame with the plop of frogs we see no

reflection of ourselves. A deep unseeing deep down
to fierce beauty. God, ourselves. Home, the walk

palms all that's been named. We look again
for the blond rabbit, petite, settled on its side, not maimed.

Three

The Everlasting Universe of Things
—Shelley

It was spring the way spring comes
so hard in places with long winter:
trees and streets were dripping with flowers.
I lived in an efficiency; I didn't have a bed.

I owned only vintage clothes: clothes
someone else had worn seemed to have a life
of their own. I gave my dresses names.
My favorite, Marilyn Monroe, was a yellow rose

print dress with rhinestones and half pearls
scattered down the flaring skirt. I had to hem it
up by hand. I must have sewed ten feet by hand.
I'll show it to you later if you want.

My place soon got too small for everything
we did. He left a note asking me to meet him
at Oakdale, the graveyard across the street.
I promised I would make it end.

Sure I'd had boys who could stay all night,
but he was like a good dessert you want again
for breakfast, like that rich sponge cake
laced with rum they eat in Italy. Tiramisu? Yes.

That hot afternoon I put on Marilyn
and walked over all those graves
full of real, I mean, rooted flowers.
I found him way in back

39

using a tombstone as a chair.
In his briefcase he had wrapped
cold white wine in a monogrammed towel.
He'd drink any time of day. We drank it

from the bottle and kissed. When we kissed
it made me think of fish and flowers.
Then he kissed down my dress with his lips
until my breasts were bare.

He spread the dress out over a grave.
It looked like a circle of light ready to be used.
After it was over, I watched him find his clothes;
he looked much older dressed.

When he was out of sight, I ran to the arboretum
nearby. It shared land with graves.
After what we had just done,
those woods seemed like a miniature wild.

I ran through the birches and the pines,
past the peony field. Marilyn flared up
around me as I ran. I ran down to the river.
I didn't care who saw me run.

The Huron's so dirty dogs won't swim in it.
I knelt on the bank to breathe, panting,
then I waded in. The water
was dark as chocolate syrup.

I kicked my sandals off and let the river take them.
Marilyn spread her skirt like a dirty flower.
When the brown water reached my chest,
I let go. That water smelled like a new dug hole.

That water had touched graves.
It felt so good, so cool, to float, but I was drifting
far downstream. I swam hard against small waves.
I passed a guy with a varnished walking stick.

Near my building, I crawled out of the river,
shook off like a dog and walked home wet.
The dress was stuck all over, wrapped tight
around me like a morning glory at night.

Aspirants and Postulants

I.

The heart out looking for something
to do. Everything holds
something, she remarks
to herself. A praying
mantis unfolds a bug. Why
think now
how Ms. So and So's lips
look when she kisses? Listen.

Slap of fishes. Water
lily skirt and
mint spring. Big wishes.

II.

So much talk. About the difference
between this and that. As if kisses could be
made with words.

If he thinks he's lost he is. *The road
here has no middle line*, he blurts
out loud and sits where center
ought to be. This is pure
astonishment. If he thinks
a word, he's in the thick of it. *Ecstasy*
up close. Logic stumbles
in the ditch.

Spume, froth, foam, scum. The reason
we're here is the reason we've come.

III.

What will the city man think
as he points his auto north today? Chicago.
Robbed flat against a chain-link fence.

This night his feet felt
over rocks—a stream that doesn't
connect to any major river or larger body
of water. The moon bruise on the elbow
of these old mountains lowed like a fog
cow in the southern night.

He thought about what lovers really want
to know: *Is my mind moving with another's?*
In the midst of memory accreting around
him he already felt sadness sidling
up to the center of experience. The others
wondered what would stick to them like burrs.
Will he say the bullfrogs rioted like taxis or will
they be just frogs calling over water? Will he see
there's no point in asking how
many snakes are in the grass?
Immersion's not enough.

IV.

How she wanted
to walk into the mangled dark, bump
into him as if into a tree that comes
alive to hold her
like a lovely trout in
flat out hands, saying *here*
I am.

V.

And what have we got
to say? That we want
to try to be good? We are
so close to coming
to love, the preword state,
to lingering in a cool, night place
which doesn't translate.

The Second Sunday of Easter

The Sunday after the lady-fluttering
carnation, rose, and orchid corsage orison
attendance is down.
A hole in the left sole of my only shoes
will not keep me from kneeling up front
for what I want
right now.

I am full of last night.
This *is* the body.
This *is* the blood.
He looked at me
as if I held the cup.
I do and I do.
Between the acts of love I fell asleep.

This spring we brought the distance
between us to the width of a light bulb filament
and we danced in that strand of light,
saying *yes*,
until we came as one.

At seventeen I palmed the host.
Like a lover who has faked too long
I decided to come clean—
to complete a moment right there and then;
I hid the disk and took it home to keep
between the mattress and box spring.

An acolyte cups his hands
under the old, old woman's hands

next to mine, forbidding the host to fall.
Why am I, invader of old rituals, here?
After ten years I can chew the past, and need,
however it comes about,
word made deed.

Something New

Cows dragging milk inside
pepper the satin folds
of valley on this drive to
drive as far as my will
will take me.

I gave up the fierce pleasure
of walking a wedding
dress to the dumpster and
let someone else buy that myth-
scratching crinoline.

I'm learning firsthand
the usefulness of art-
ifacts: buttercream ribbon
ties up sugar snap peas—
they'd wrap around anything
unmoving. A veil undone
guards twelve blushing
berry bushes. New gold
can crown even wisdom teeth.

Here, finally, the inn of enough
firm old American sensuality—watersilk
walls and windows higher than three
of me. I like the sound of wood
floors planking under Persian.
I like the porter asking
"Everything all right, ma'am?"—
wondering when I became a ma'am.

This bed is a ship. No
sacred bean beneath will poke
my solo sleep I float on
like a lily in the bridal suite.

A Small Red Parcel

No true love tattoos, kites, or funnel cakes—
the Bearded Clam
is closed. A seatless wheel, gold band around the sun,
will finger Assateague, one mile away, where
wild ponies with manes like sheaves
of string do bite and kick.

Handholders swing the V
they make
as if they could catch something falling
between them. The partner understands
what the innkeeper understands:
occupancy means ease.

Two persons with metal detectors pass their wands
over the sand for the one the waves
slipped off when the woman, the man slid under.
They do their work, don't they?
How much they think is swept up,
under, or away. The waves will ease
another load tonight.

They wash a find off in the sea, slip it on
their thumbs, stop, sell up, or
clink it in the find box under the seat.
Object detected makes sleep beep through their heads.

Imagine, hyperbole reneged, none that got
away, hope paying off, in gold, of course.

The coupling of work and sea will present
to them, sweetly, in no words at all.
Much will be given up and only for their taking.

You Are Given an Amulet

An amulet is a metaphoric trap for an unknown future.
An amulet destroys what wants to destroy you. An amulet
is good for as long as the objects in the amulet exist.
When the objects go, the words held in them are gone.
    CHRISTOPHER DAVIS ROBERTS, anthropologist

Piece of the sole of a cowboy boot of someone
who has crossed a fast stream
by jumping on rocks without looking back.

Part of wire rim glasses that flew off the dashboard
and out the window of a jeep going at least fifty-five
and were never found by their owner, who was
on his way to see a woman for the last time.

A smallsize freshwater crab claw found by a swimmer,
underwater, while she was thinking of how
a certain man's index finger
smelled of cigarettes and lilac vegetal.

Slice of lipstick (color: "Almost Red") lost
under the farthest back booth at Nick's
during a thirty-minute conversation between
a woman and a man who left in the same direction.

Soil from where the shadow fell of two bodies, embracing,
who knew what they were. Who knew
that opposite sides of the same thing
cannot endure the difficulty
of seeing their lost half found and held.

Sliver of a thirty-inch narrow-mouthed glass jug

that a man and a woman lay next to on the brown linoleum
of a strange apartment while making love before
it started to rain and he went out softly.
Without closing the door.

A Z_{10} *piece from a Scrabble game* a woman found
in a dryer at the Spin Out laundromat in a new town.

Four

An Appalachian Town:
Points of Definition

This is the town to mumble down
the ungarnished streets of kindness.
Bells like marbles dropped in a pail
give you the time downtown.

This is the town to forget you found
a bush or cave or secret spot.
No chocolate pig hides outside;
only stray dogs sniff at the ground.

This is the town that understands room:
a cup fits inside a bowl inside a pot,
a poke in dough should leave a hole,
and love is the fall between who and whom.

Delilah in Dixie

The malted-milk girl stands up to ride
her pink five-speed uphill. Her brown hair
ponies behind her as she
clips past her own house, cuts
the corner; her dad yells her name, but
he's too late. She's got her way to go
as far as the town will take her.

The beer-belly man combs his Rototiller
through the garden that could feed us all.
He's been untangling his plot since March.
His Spanish mossy beard and hair could use a trim.

Now his wife follows with a brown paper bag.
She yanks two weeds, steps out,
slides off her scarf, and
furrows hands through fresh hair
as though this were her first luxury.

Now our man stops his machine and lights
a pile of hairy brush, steps back surprised
at big heat on this first real shortsleeve day.
He plops down his bushel-basket belly, lights
one up, and smokes in little ratted puffs.

His boy, a real fatso (What does that family eat?
Everything that grows, I suppose), rolls out a tire.
Each step makes hair hit his back like old horse rope.
I will go down and have a word
if he sets that tire on fire.

He rolls the tire
up to his father's knees. The mother doesn't see
because she's pulling weeds, filling
a bag with messy pigweed.

Males run their hands over balding tread,
reading calm decision. Now our girl curls
into the picture, pedals panting
under my balcony, yells, *Hey,*
you with the hair on your head,
why don't you ever come out to play?

July's Tune

What do you want to do?
The plumes are drooping on our cockatoos.
Even the squirrels are spooling
around branches like gray crewel.
The faux English garden is in ruin.
What do you want to do?
Tonight, even the moon
is hot. I know you'd rather swim in a pool,
but let's climb the dunes and cool
off in the ocean. Let's go nude.
Fine! We'll play by all the rules.
Would you rather sit and stew?
I can't wave an ice cold wand, what do you want to do?

Working Out in the New South

On the sweatshop stair machine I read junk
about who and hair and food. It makes me feel
part of the culture I pretend
I just landed in, where I got fat
from love. Almond cake melts off of me—the calorie
clock says I burned 400. My time's intention—
is there now less of me?

On the cover this woman looks like Auschwitz—an earth
alien shaved serious, looking for home
on the tone machines. I flip the slick pages
as though this were my job, pedal faster, remembering
what a plush life I now live. I love
my work. I am buying a brick cottage
as old as my grandmother. It has fire-
places and built-in bookshelves and will be a child-free
pleasure dome. Sometimes I like to think
American and claim I make the life I live,
but most of the time I feel plain lucky.

The tiffanies flanking me sweat out something
else. They're held in place by pink spandex and strong hair spray.
Will they undo the form that makes them? I work hard
at other things. If they notice me they don't show it here
or in the locker room where they cream themselves and talk
shop with the mirror: husbands, kids,
how many gained or lost.

I give in for the day, strip off my paint-

flecked T-shirt, turn the fake
sauna up to ten, ready to
take some heat in the South.

Carnivores

Bud is marrow-old and dry as hung meat jerky.
He grows green things that eat for anyone
to buy, take home, incorporate.
Our Saturday couple eats up his handmade signs
and laughs at them for miles:
they've been taken in by the real
South—the emollient South, by words that ingest
like textual sex. Our man's waiting inside

for them, relishing pink morning. All morning
they've been wrapped around their wish.
Each adores the other, wants a green feast
of another's best body, light, and seed.
Now inside, our couple eyes butterworts,
sundews, pitcher plants, and Venus traps suckling
on the little light he lets in. "Don't shut the traps!" snaps
a penciled sign nailed over eighty open jaws.

Our man bristles when they drop a bug
down a cobra's flesh-green gullet.
They feel the pale air closing in: a panic of recycling.
Time now to get their money's worth,

but what to buy and what to leave?
They love the red drops waiting
on the sundew's baby feet. Bud lays it in an open box.
At home, they grill steak, wait for the plant to eat.

Vulgar Joy

A couple, not married to each other,
will walk savanna plains—
the only place on earth
where Venus flytraps plant themselves.
They'll say they're looking
for carnivorous plants growing wild in the woods.
Lone men, planking over the brackish mucilage,
will pass the worried couple in the woods,
look down, and tell them something without words.
Their guidebook will tell them,
The size of the prey depends on that of the trap.

She'll know where to leave the path,
to step off the wooden walk
on ground turned dark and moist as snakes.
She will kneel on loam.
There, she'll find the pretty traps.
He will stand above her like a tree. *He should
be kneeling here with me*, she'll think.
Instead, he's looking down at me.
The sizzle of "what now" will pour thick
in the plashy instant brining.

She'll take a twig to tease
a little set of jaws to close
the teeth that mesh on greening lobes.
Other will meet other
and size up sticky possibility.
Venus's nectar will bead the trap;
let grace dissolve the rest.

Eating Angels

In the year everyone became interested
in angels, I saw clearly
things people use to find
familiar hosts. I learned this
in semiprivate, a hospital room I shared with a holy
mother who'd live to tell how I hit
a deer with my motorcycle mowing fast.

Strangers who had heard the story
poked their caps into the room
to get a look at me. They said
someone in a rusty pick-up truck took
the buck away to dress and eat
as accidental food. I couldn't recall
the crash, but when I slept I flew.

My *Sound of Music* husband would be
back some other day. It didn't matter much:
I was lonely with him anywhere. He was
stretching polymers in the lab, gnawing
a rack of beef off a smoking baking sheet,
or making time downtown. He had
almost loved me once or twice.

My roommate's country western family filled
the room, cut meat for me, and ate
the red jello I offered. The son,
a fat cherub who clearly saved
my life, fit himself into an angle, a corner to lament
his recent losses: cows he loved, sold
first for money, then for food:

Min, Clayette, and my Little Red One.
To pass the time I put the names in all
possible orders, but his still sounded
best. I remembered
something
when the country western family left.
They thought I was nice and called me *honey, sugar.*

Maybe they understood
about flapless wings;
I wanted to go home,
throw my things
in paper bags and walk away alone.
I would forget what I couldn't remember.
Temporarily humbled, I thought

I could simply sew up the holes
and lift off the second I was vertical,
but I had hit headfirst.
Now, I see
I was hardly harmed.
Alive again, I am friendly
to any angels looking for me.

Something Evermore About To Be

I.
With fur and teeth the pushy guests moved in.
They gnawed the skin from pears set out for show
and ticked all night across the attic beams
above the couple's wedding bed. Outdoors
they ate the seed hung up for wrens and jays.
One night both saw six tails dip down and gleam,
so plastic pink like fleshy things in dreams.

II.
Shhh! See them at work, content as mammals?
They're setting up a big aquarium.
Is it the aqua calm that takes her in
or is it the vegetative rhythm?
She wants so much to make something with him.
Each day of eight months married makes new love.
She said she'd never wed again. *Enough's*
enough! He made her dream of dolphins
and held her hand in sleep, then she gave in.

III.
By day, the cat they bought will dream in fish;
by night, the cat will use its natural gifts.

Five

A Celibate Imagination

Hi! I don't care about your actual uncle
in his skull and sweet snuff,
the rat-eyed rat in his root cellar
and real spots on his beeches,
red spruces, and papery birches.
I, too, could love his ethnic ink.

Where does your imagination make love
with the world that's always anyway you?
When you abandon the restoration of the real,
wrap cords around the necks of power tools,
where does your imagination rain,
over Uncle Anton's miter box?

O sad times washed in acid!
You can't help but live inside your life,
even when you step outside
in stockings oily with lanolin
of the sheep that bore them,
even when you step outside in horror.

Incarnation Café

My view is the side slice: ant farm,
agate, rocket ship. But you,
my pearl, my cashew, my comfort,
are the outside of inside,
cat pads and horn velvet,
the aqua calm of shadows hammered down.

When I look up into the elegant,
past plastic chandeliers,
I spy something with a name.
And it doesn't fall on chocolate cake
and it doesn't dust our napes.
It flexes like a femur.

Desire Lines

I'm a snail moving across sandpaper,
and an elephant in long, hard labor.
I'm an unthread shiny needle,
also a white cake top in the freezer,
and I'm iris bulbs in a sack,
yet I'm a head without a hat.
I'm baby corn,
and a red lipstick nobody's worn;
I'm a small plot on the moon,
and engines shining in showrooms.
I'm a fresh baseball white in a box,
and an empty stringer tied to the dock.
I'm sheets snapping like kites,
also an eggtooth ready to bite.
But I'm the little wings on penguins,
and the no-name horse who'll win.
I'm a dewlap poking out—
have you guessed what I'm about?
I tell you I'm thick wool on a sheep,
and I'm dreams that last past sleep.

Things Oracular

Let them think it's night
and sing awhile
behind the velvet drape,
then stop. Let them
tuck their fine plumed heads like hats
and sleep the sleep of the sexless.
Let them wake up
where the mirror was
and peck invisible tarn.
Let them kiss all day
with beaks like little pliers
squeaking on an ingot.
Let them preen and preen,
bow to one another
and practice bowing and bow
like fussy queens.

Emanation

Pink foxglove, gardenia in ivory
charmeuse and ruffled lady's mantle:
I woke up in a female world—
not my idea of the female world.

I deadhead the fuss of everyday
marigolds, grown for rapid color bath,
and cut back the easy ivy. So. So.
Sunday's thin straps slip down like a sheath's.

The garden wall around me is ballast
saved from ships. A civil war was fought.
Its dead live down the street. From here I see
their white stone slabs as awkward as pulled teeth.

I could die here or here, so I tend to things:
small live things are far away,
all live things are far away.
One learns to live with the chattering dead.

Anoles dewlap as they now copulate
on the garden gate. They are themselves abstract.
Their shrill red melon gorging moves me not.
I'm quite content to be a mammal.

I want to live among others and objects.
It behooves me to find a way
inside. Where is the voice
that is the words and does not wear them?

Outside the inside begins with a vine.
A slap of old and calm and cold
over what you hold
and what you hold.

Objects all around you take on light.
The dark and sexed and godless self,
now lustrates in light
and comes, at last, to light.

Kathleen Halme's poetry manuscript *The Everlasting Universe of Things* was selected by Edward Hirsch as winner of the 1994 North Carolina Writers' Network Harperprints Chapbook Competition. She completed her MFA in Creative Writing at the University of Michigan, where her work was awarded the Hopwood Creative Writing Award. Halme is a recipient of a National Endowment for the Humanities Grant, scholarships to Breadloaf and Sewanee Writers' Conferences, and an Emerging Artists' Grant from the Arts Council of the Lower Cape Fear. She lives in Wilmington, North Carolina, and is an assistant professor at the University of North Carolina at Wilmington, where she teaches creative writing.

The Contemporary Poetry Series

EDITED BY PAUL ZIMMER

Dannie Abse, *One–Legged on Ice*
Susan Astor, *Dame*
Gerald Barrax, *An Audience of One*
Tony Connor, *New and Selected Poems*
Franz Douskey, *Rowing Across the Dark*
Lynn Emanuel, *Hotel Fiesta*
John Engels, *Vivaldi in Early Fall*
John Engels, *Weather–Fear: New and Selected Poems, 1958–1982*
Brendan Galvin, *Atlantic Flyway*
Brendan Galvin, *Winter Oysters*
Michael Heffernan, *The Cry of Oliver Hardy*
Michael Heffernan, *To the Wreakers of Havoc*
Conrad Hilberry, *The Moon Seen as a Slice of Pineapple*
X. J. Kennedy, *Cross Ties*
Caroline Knox, *The House Party*
Gary Margolis, *The Day We Still Stand Here*
Michael Pettit, *American Light*
Bin Ramke, *White Monkeys*
J. W. Rivers, *Proud and on My Feet*
Laurie Sheck, *Amaranth*
Myra Sklarew, *The Science of Goodbyes*
Marcia Southwick, *The Night Won't Save Anyone*
Mary Swander, *Succession*
Bruce Weigl, *The Monkey Wars*
Paul Zarzyski, *The Make–Up of Ice*

The Contemporary Poetry Series

EDITED BY BIN RAMKE